HEALTH & WELL-BEING

For The Professional Driver

by
Professional Driver
Brian Roberts

AuthorHouse™ UK Ltd.
1663 Liberty Drive
Bloomington, IN 47403 USA
www.authorhouse.co.uk
Phone: 0800.197.4150

© 2015, 2016 Brian Roberts. All rights reserved.

No part of this book may be reproduced, stored in a retrieval system, or
transmitted by any means without the written permission of the author.

Published by AuthorHouse 04/17/2016

ISBN: 978-1-5049-3916-4 (sc)
ISBN: 978-1-5049-3917-1 (e)

Any people depicted in stock imagery provided by Thinkstock are models,
and such images are being used for illustrative purposes only.
Certain stock imagery © Thinkstock.

Because of the dynamic nature of the Internet, any web addresses or links contained in this book may have changed
since publication and may no longer be valid. The views expressed in this work are solely those of the author and do
not necessarily reflect the views of the publisher, and the publisher hereby disclaims any responsibility for them.

authorHOUSE®

Acknowledgements

Go-Ahead London General Putney Head Office, London, England – Public Relations Staff: Thank you to **Mr Sheldon Malcolm and his team** for allowing filming on the company's vehicles and for their support and encouragement.

Posture Illustration

Many thanks to Camberwell Garage drivers for their time and support - Mr Arjan Meta, Mr Comoe-Desire Kouadio, Miss Karla Golichova, Miss Anita Lisbie, Mr Joseph A B Sesay, Mr Balvindar Singh and Mr W M Wong.

Book Development

Book cover designer: R A Graphics

Illustration pictures taken from www.pixabay.com

Conclusion bus picture taken in London Transport Museum, Covent Garden Piazza, London, WC2E 7BB

Initial proof reading and editing: Marrietta Grant-Silvera. She is the author for the forthcoming book 'Comfort Through Adversity'. Should be a fabulous read; be sure to get a copy.

Final proof reading and editing: Gillian Barry BSc PG Dip MSc MBACP

Author's final words

The year 2014 marked over 100 years of motorised buses for Transport for London, where many celebrations of activities took place for the drivers and the general public.

I am delighted to present this book at such a significant time. It will be rewarding for the transport industry to promote this book making it available to all the drivers.

Contents

INTRODUCTION	1
CHAPTER 1 - THE TRANSPORT INDUSTRY AND THE DRIVER'S HEALTH	
The Industry	2
Occupational Hazards	3
CHAPTER 2 - DRIVING POSTURE	
Which Driving Posture Do I Use?	4
Correcting Your Driving Posture	6
CHAPTER 3 - THE IMPACT OF EXERCISE ON YOUR HEALTH AND WELLNESS	
Author Brian Roberts Gives His View	8
CHAPTER 4 - COMMON AILMENTS OF DRIVERS AND HOW TO PREVENT THEM	
Stress	10
Driving Back Pain	15
Musculature Disorders	19
Nutritional Aid Chart	23
Gastrointestinal Disorders	26
Cardiovascular Disorders	30
CHAPTER 5 - EATING HEALTHY AT WORK	
Emotional Eating and Weight Gain	33
Correct Chewing For Your Digestive System	34
Microwave Reheating - Good or Bad? You Decide!	36
CHAPTER 6 - SOCIAL HEALTH AND ADDICTION	
Cigarette Smoking and Alcohol	38
Alcohol and Drug Consumption	39
NUTRITIONAL AID CENTRE PAGE FOLD	
CHAPTER 7 - CONCLUSION	41
SUGGESTED READING	42
REFERENCES	43

Health and Well-Being

INTRODUCTION

It is well known that professional driving is one of the most hazardous occupations to a person's health. This landmark handbook for Professional Driver's health and well-being, should be embraced and treated as a key element to remaining healthy in this challenging career.

This manual addresses some ailments that are commonly encountered by Professional Drivers. In exploring the causes of these disorders, readers will be introduced to data from numerous surveys, reports and analyses, some of which have been archived. These compelling facts are included to enable you to understand the challenges that professional driving poses to the driver's health.

The provided recommendations address some of the most common complaints and advise how to avoid injury or illness. Illustrations, literature and pictures demonstrate the correct and safe driving posture, provide proposals to avoiding stress and demonstrate exercises that can help prevent the most common driving related ailments. The exercises are illustrated in a bus but other industry professionals will need to use an alternative space. Vital tips will help you examine your eating habits at work and help you to determine if they are endangering your health. A Nutritional Aid Chart is enclosed to help heal and prevent possible oversights in the future.

Readers will discover why Government Guidelines play such an important role in the transportation industry while examining social health and addiction. The various elements of addiction explored in this book are presented with clarity, in easily understood terms.

In addition to the need of this guide for the Professional Driver's health, this handbook will investigate the commitment of the transport industry to sustaining a healthy driving force.

Health and Well-Being

CHAPTER 1

THE TRANSPORT INDUSTRY AND THE DRIVER'S HEALTH

The Industry

The driving industry has grown tremendously since the turn of the century. The roads are now used more than ever for the transportation of goods. The consequence is increased congestion on our roads.

Delivery of home products has become fashionable. Most companies, large and small, now offer these services.

The turn of the 21st century has seen a surge in online shopping, resulting in an increased demand for delivery trucks and vans.

This has increased the demand for Professional Drivers.

Today, more people are holidaying and sightseeing, increasing the demand for coaches and buses.

Transport for London (TfL) has added numerous bus routes, due to high demand throughout the city and towns. In fact, 2013 saw an increase in usage of both bus and rail services in the UK. It is felt this may be partly due to the significant increase in fuel costs, forcing many commuters to seek a cheaper alternative.

With the recession still upon us and an increased number of people out of work, the unemployed transport discount pass has led to a dramatic increase in commuters using public transport.

Health and Well-Being

Occupational Hazards

Delivery of products or services normally require human intervention. Someone has to drive the vehicle that delivers the products to the consumers or the commuters to their destinations.

Research has shown that driving is one of the most hazardous occupations for one's health. Drivers have higher rates of cardiovascular, gastrointestinal and musculature disorders than other occupations.

Drivers are exposed to a number of health problems as a direct result of their posture whilst driving. Sitting in the driving position exerts considerable pressure on the spine and can cause a number of problems to the musculature system; in particular backaches, neck strain, muscle injury and general stiffness.

John Whitelegg (1995) reported: *"A driver being constantly subjected to road noise is another cause of poor health. Noise can damage hearing and result in a number of psychological problems that can contribute to stress. Noise contributes to disorders of the cardiovascular, nervous and digestive system. These areas of the body are prone to be attacked in Professional Drivers. Without diagnosis, drivers work under ill health, which causes inefficiency.*

As internal and external noise is experienced by the driver at the same time as vibration from the engine, there is a combined pressure on the Professional Driver's well-being."

3

Health and Well-Being

CHAPTER 2

DRIVING POSTURE

Which Driving Posture Do I Use?

There is concern that many drivers are prone to serious injuries as a result of adopting faulty sitting postures whilst driving. Considering the fact that maintaining the correct position for driving is important, a large percentage of motorists knew of the pitfalls, yet continued to drive without adjusting their vehicle seat and controls to help their body achieve the best driving posture. This is partly due to lack of information regarding the possible outcome.

Study these postures presently adopted by Professional Drivers:

ILLUSTRATION 1

Window Screen Driver

Points to notice
The driver is leaning forward and sits with an arched back, legs and arms are bent and he is gripping the top of the steering wheel.

Injuries consist of:
Shoulder pain, forming a hunched back and early onset of fatigue.

Solution
Relax; tense and nervous drivers are most likely to adopt this position, leading to tense shoulders, so try to avoid situations that cause tension.

ILLUSTRATION 2

Office Driver

Points to notice
The driver has a straight back, bent arms and one hand on the steering wheel, leaving the other hand free, which could lead to distraction with mobile phone or paperwork etc.

Injuries consist of:
Headaches, eye strain, feet cramps and pain in the coccyx. The coccyx is the last bone of the spine.

Solution
Stay focused, avoid doing other things with hands whilst driving and keep both hands on the steering wheel. If required, when safe to do, adjust your seating position to help ease the strain on your coccyx. Move feet regularly to encourage circulation.

Health and Well-Being

ILLUSTRATION 3

Couch Potato

Points to notice
The driver has straight arms, an inclined seat, straight legs and a low driving position.

Injuries consist of:
Side aches and lumbar pain. Lumbar pain will be felt from the lower back ribs to the buttock.

Solution
Beware of low seating and slumping back into an over reclined seat. Position your seat high. Your knees should not be higher than your hips; this reminds you to sit up.

ILLUSTRATION 4

Poser

Points to notice
The driver's seat is reclined, his arm is on the window ledge or outside the window and he has one hand on the wheel. Drivers adopting this position are usually young men and women.

Injuries consist of:
Arm and shoulder aches from resting on the window ledge and pain in the lateral oblique muscles and abdominals.

Solution
Sit in an upright position with knees lower than hips. You should be able to reach the accelerator and brake pedals without stretching your legs.

Health and Well-Being

Correcting Your Driving Posture

There is almost twice as much pressure on your back when you sit incorrectly, than when you sit properly, so posture while driving is very important. Maintaining a good, relaxed position will help reduce stress on the spine. You will also be less likely to suffer from fatigue.

Here are some tips to help you prepare yourself in the driver's seat:

Do Not Wear Tight Clothing While Driving

Tight clothing can impede your driving by restricting your body movements and blood flow. It can also cause you to feel uncomfortable and make it harder to relax properly.

Watch Your Knees

As you sit in the seat, look at the seat inclination, your knees should be lower than your hips and at an angle that will allow comfortable access to the pedals. Make sure you do not over extend the knees in order to reach the pedals.

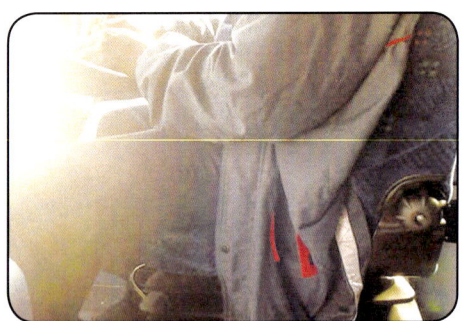

Position of the Back Rest

The back rest of the seat should be at an 80-85 degree angle, allowing for a slight tilt to the top end of the back rest. This will aid your spine when sitting, as this is the natural spine position. Sitting with a straight back rest can put severe pressure on the coccyx.

Arms Bent at 9:15 o'clock Position on the Steering Wheel

Adjust the steering wheel towards you to ensure that your arms are bent and at the 9:15 o'clock wheel position. Also ensure that you are as close to the steering wheel as possible, without compromising your sense of safety. Make sure that you can reach the control knobs, without over extending your arms or leaning forward. If you habitually sit too far away, you can develop or aggravate back pain.

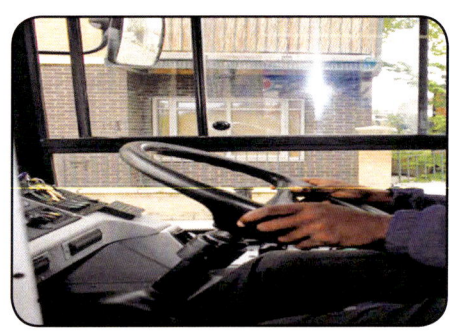

Health and Well-Being

Sit up Straight

No matter how relaxed you may be, avoid sinking into the driving seat. You need to maintain a high position at all times, keeping your shoulders wide and your head held high. Sinking down into the seat, slouching forward or leaning slightly to the side are unhealthy driving positions. These postures can adversely affect your spinal alignment and make you prone to back injuries.

Keep Your Foot Over The Pedal

It is important to keep your foot centred when driving. The foot should be on the pedal with the heel firmly placed near the bottom end. When applying pressure to the pedal, it is essential that you use the toe of the foot, keeping the heel firmly in place. This will enable the whole foot to do the work, putting less tension on the Achilles tendon. The Achilles tendon is a tough band of fibrous tissue that connects the calf muscles to the heel bone (calcaneus).

Health and Well-Being

CHAPTER 3

THE IMPACT OF EXERCISE ON YOUR HEALTH AND WELLNESS

Author Brian Roberts stated the following about attaining health and wellness through daily exercise:

"I have a great deal of experience in fitness and well-being. My previous profession was in the leisure and recreation industry, where I held a management position managing various coaching staff, as well as Weight Watchers representatives. I was also active in organising many events and promoting health and wellness. These included events such as Jog & Stretch, which provided joggers with a full length stretch after jogging, as it improved the awareness of joggers about the importance of stretching, in order to prevent cramps and promote flexibility."

Your energy level will increase as you introduce more movement into your daily routine. That's one of the benefits of daily exercise.

Exercise can take place in any surrounding.

There is no need for Lycra outfits and track suits. You can do every day exercises just as you are. Daily exercise can come in many forms, such as walking, doing step ups, carrying heavy shopping, using the stairs etc.

Anything that gets your muscles working, your joints moving and your heart pumping faster can be considered as exercise. It should fit nicely into your lifestyle, doing a little bit as you go about your daily chores. As little as half an hour of exercise a day can enhance your well-being. You can exercise in 5 minute slots or as long as you choose (although ideally it should be in one block to be most effective). Above all, **you should make a start and feel how it works for you.**

The UK Government back in 1999 initiated a Cycle to Work Scheme to assist employers in keeping a healthy work force.

(G-AL) Bus Talk (Issue 26) excerpt report:

"In February 2014 Go-Ahead London (G-AL) launched a Cycle to Work scheme, where employees had the opportunity to apply for up to £1,000 for a bike and associated equipment, financed by a salary deduction arrangement. Nearly 200 bikes have been ordered, valued at around £14,000, since its recent launch. Not only does the scheme help to keep participants fit, but it also reduces carbon emission."

Health and Well-Being

G-AL is committed to keeping drivers healthy and this is just one of its projects to achieve this goal. Bicycles at the Camberwell Green drivers bike lookup.

Many people today, decide to cycle to work and for leisure, making use of the Barclay Bike Hiring Scheme. This is the latest Government initiative which provides the dual service of daily exercise along with cost effective travel, creating a healthier community. In 2015 the Government teamed up with Santander keeping the hiring scheme in operation. It's proving to be very popular.

Government Guidelines suggest 30 minutes of exercise daily, 5 days a week is enough to prevent the risk of heart disease, diabetes and other related illnesses; it will also enhance your mind, reduce obesity and boost your spirit.

If your aim is to feel healthier and look better, there is no need to do the kind of exercise that leaves you out of breath and sweating profusely. You just need to elevate your heart rate for 20 minutes continuously for your exercise regime to have the most benefit.

Health Warning!

Remember your limitations when exercising. Be conscious of how far you are pushing yourself, ensuring you refrain from doing too much, too soon. Exercise passionately but with caution, making sure that you continue to breathe throughout each motion, without undue strain.

If you are on medication or have health issues, consult a medical professional prior to attempting any exercises. Show them the exercises you intend to attempt from this manual.

Health and Well-Being

CHAPTER 4

COMMON AILMENTS OF DRIVERS AND HOW TO PREVENT THEM

Stress

Being under stress is far from enjoyable. It increases the challenges of driving, as it raises your level of anxiety. It is difficult for stressed out drivers to enjoy their work. The joy of driving past iconic places such as Big Ben, Trafalgar Square, London Eye and similar landmarks eludes the stressed out driver.

There is joy in working outdoors and having responsibility for all who board your vehicle as long as you are in a good frame of mind. This industry offers the additional bonus of boosting your income by working frequently available overtime. Keep in mind, however, that driving more than a 7 day shift may not be conducive to your health.

The high availability of overtime exists mainly as a result of a considerable level of absenteeism due to stress or related illnesses. There is also a high level of staff turnover due to driver burnout, also caused by stress.

Many studies have been done on the effects of stress and driving, to the extent to which these studies highlight the same concerns: high demands, low control and low support. The combination of these three factors can lead to stress and consequently, an increased risk of physical and mental occupational illnesses. This leads to absenteeism and decreased productivity of employees in enterprises.

When assessing the varying stress triggers that a Professional Driver faces, it is no wonder that before long, drivers start showing signs of stress.

Health and Well-Being

Prevention of stress is ultimately in the driver's hands. They must ensure that they are fit and healthy to deal with the pressure of the

industry. The required skills in this profession vary from mastering difficult manoeuvres to driving in dangerous weather. Your reactions are as vitally important, as your level of alertness and observation. It is therefore imperative that drivers get enough sleep.

The Driving Standards Agency (DSA 2013) recommends that drivers observe their sleep patterns, to ensure that they are fit to drive. An excerpt from this recommendation states,

"Recognise if your normal sleep patterns have been disrupted, for example by having to care for children or when on night or rotating shifts,

and be aware of where this may affect your driving ability.
Being tired, before or during your journey, affects your ability to drive safely.

a) *A poor seating position and bad posture can make you tired.*

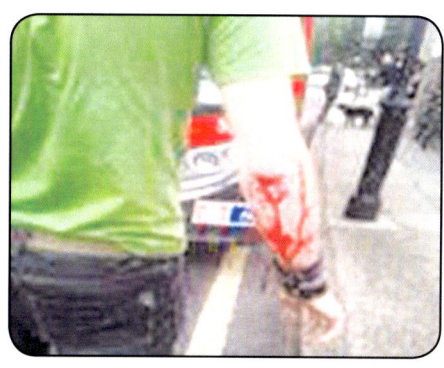

b) *A poor diet, or eating food at the wrong time, can make you more likely to fall asleep.*
c) *There are times of the day when we are all likely to feel more tired."*

The DSA stress how easily it is for tiredness to creep into your day. If you are tired, it will adversely affect your driving ability and your level of patience. As a strategy, have by your side aromatherapy oils. You would be amazed by the benefits of a rub of lavender essential oil applied to the tip of your shirt collar or stub of tie. It provides instant relief when feeling stressed, tired or restless.

{Do not apply the oil to your skin}.

Ylang-ylang, peppermint, lavender, rosemary and jasmine are all essential oils that give an instant uplift. Be sure to keep one handy.

Health and Well-Being

Kompier, (1996) includes the following:

High and conflicting demands - Passengers, time pressure and safety

"The task of the driver is mentally demanding because they have to cope with conflicting requests. The company and the public want the driver to maintain good contact with passengers and to be service oriented, for instance: Providing information to travellers (such as information about timetables, routes, stops, fares, etc).

These are also important aspects of job satisfaction. In the operator's daily life, the demand for service by the individual passenger often conflicts with the need to keep to a tight schedule in dense traffic. The third demand on the driver, the demand to drive safely and follow traffic regulations, also often conflicts with the other two."

Health and Well-Being

Recommended Exercises With Illustrations

Deep Breathing Exercise

Get in a relaxed position and start by focusing on your breathing. Breathe slowly but deeply. Breathe in slowly through your nose and then breathe out slowly through your mouth.
Draw air deep into your abdomen. Feel your abdomen getting tight as you fill your lungs with air.

Now that you are breathing slowly, begin to count your breaths. Breathe in through your nose to the count of 5 and then slowly exhale through your mouth to the count of 5. Continue for at least 2 minutes.

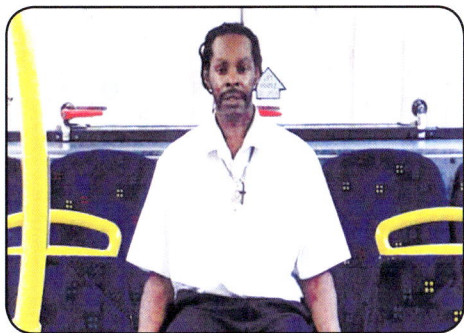

Repeat this exercise whenever you can.

Notice how relaxed you can make yourself feel just by performing this simple deep breathing exercise.

Neck, Shoulder And Head Massage

Help soothe tense muscles in the neck, shoulders and head by giving yourself a brief massage, but make sure it's not a mindless massage. For the full de-stressing benefits, stop what you are doing and be aware of the muscle tension you feel.

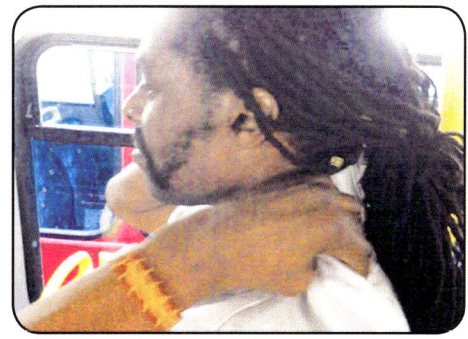

Lightly apply pressure to the tense or cramped muscles using the tips of your fingers. The cramped muscle may initially feel lumpy, as you move your fingers around the area. As you work the tension out, your pain should ease and your mind should become more settled.

Health and Well-Being

Do this whenever you can; it is a great stimulant for the mind and upper body.

Quick Body Scan

You can begin at the feet and work your way up to your head, noting and releasing any tension as you go. A thorough body scan meditation might last around 10 minutes but you can quickly complete the exercise in a minute or less as a way of relaxing and unwinding.

To help quiet your mind and boost awareness of the sensations in your body, sit or lie down in a comfortable position and close your eyes. Start by drawing your attention to individual parts of your body (back, legs, chest, shoulders etc) and check how they feel.

Health and Well-Being

Driving Back Pain

Driving involves sitting, often for extended periods of time. This static seated position can make muscles tight and sore.

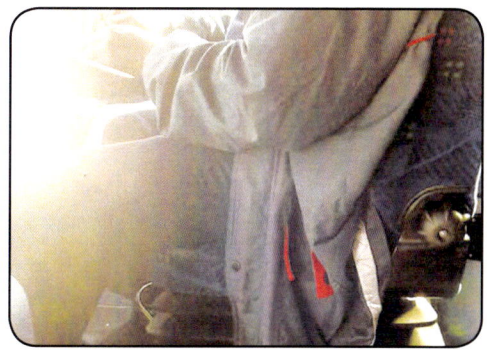

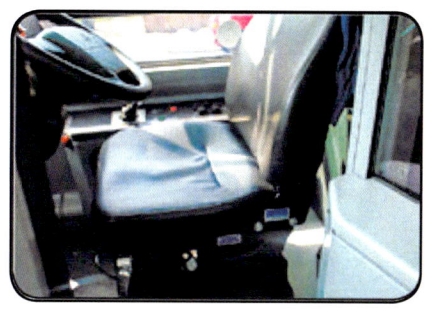

Oxygen deprivation can occur, which can lead to back pain. This oxygen deprivation can be caused by long periods of sitting in a vehicle. The seated position dramatically increases lumbar spinal pressure, as it is certainly not conducive to good lower body circulation.

Driving also involves excessive reaching and head movement. This can set the stage for muscular pain, especially when other stress

Tyre pressures that are properly set can also be beneficial. Vehicle manufacturers are always looking for more ways to achieve steady impact of the spine base. The Automotive and Commerce Vehicle Design Industry has made great advancements in cabin and seat design. Results from past research into musculature stress and muscle fatigue have led to an improvement in the driver cockpit layout. Research has revealed a particular bus may be driven by different drivers within a specific time frame. The great variation in driver size, within the driver population; demands that there be a wide range of adjustment options to accommodate these differences in driver size, weight and shape. There has been a big drive to provide more ergonomic seats, along with greater adjustability in knob controls.

factors are involved. These other stress factors include driving in bad weather, in heavy traffic or when you are late.

When sitting for prolonged periods, it is important to sit in such a way that the 'S' bend of the spinal column curvature is retained so that the spine stacks effortlessly. Vehicle vibration and rough roads increase the rate of fluid loss from the discs that compose the spinal column. Modern well sprung seats absorb some of this vibration.

Early model: Adjustable controls

Health and Well-Being

More recent model: Adjustable controls

Previous research using computer modelling, has positioned the industry to ensure a comfortable sitting position, even for persons who are particularly short or tall. All these provisions optimally position coach and bus drivers for proper alignment and comfort in their work area, by simply adjusting their seat and steering wheel in relation to their body.

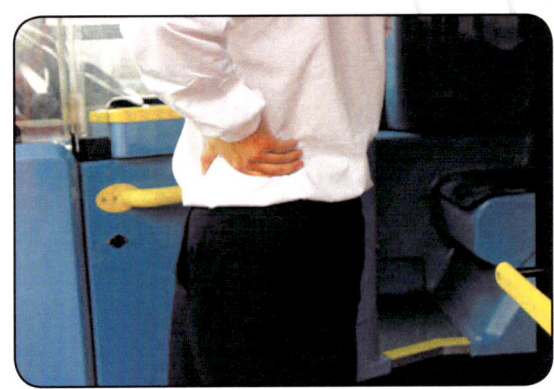

Back Pain - Why?

You must analyse your pain and attempt to determine what is causing your suffering. Is it sitting in general, operating the vehicle's pedals or the stress of traffic? Maybe you dread the shift of your job or even returning home at night to an unhappy family situation.

Historical Back Pain Prevention

Think back to basics first! Early civilizations didn't often sit, certainly not as much as we do today! Instead, they squatted to talk with friends and acquaintances, prepare and eat food, go to the lavatory, deliver babies and just about anything else you can think of doing.

Squatting aids the lumbar discs. This has the beneficial effect of pulling the spinal segments apart and sucking in fluid to plump up the discs again, thus ensuring that the spine performs at its best.

Health and Well-Being

Recommended Exercises With Illustration

Squatting needs to be an essential part of any driver's daily exercise routine, particularly when a permanently aching back hovers in the background throughout your working day. When this is the case, you need to do a couple of spinal decompression exercises as an integral part of your daily exercise routine.

Spinal decompression should be done both throughout your driving day and at the end of your day behind the wheel. Ideally, drivers should squat at intervals of every two hours (or more often if you are stiffening again).

Supportive Squat Exercise

Standing up straight, place your feet a little more than shoulder width apart, with your hips directly over knees and your knees over your ankles. Roll your shoulders back and down away from your ears.

Note: Allowing your back to bend or slouch will cause unnecessary stress on the lower back.

Extend your arms out straight so they are parallel with the ground, palms facing down as you grip a bar (or an equivalent) for added support and comfort.

Initiate movement by inhaling into the belly, pushing your buttocks backward while unlocking the hips and slightly bringing your body down. Keep pushing your hips backward as the knees begin to bend.

When the butt starts to stick out, make sure your chest and shoulders stay upright and your back stays straight. Bend forward with your hips, not your back.

Let the hip joint squat lower to the ground than your knees, but ONLY if comfortable.

You may also hear a crunching noise around the kneecap because this area has not stretched in a while! Hold this position for several seconds.

Engage your core muscles (abdominals and lateral obliques) and exhale while driving through the heels to return to standing. Imagine that your feet are stuck to the floor.

Health and Well-Being

Knees to Chest

Lie on your back with your knees slightly bent. Bring one knee up and pull it gently into your chest for 5 seconds. Repeat up to 5 times on each side.

Glute Bridge

1. Starting Phase: Lie on your back at the rear of the vehicle in a bent knee position with your feet flat on the surface. Place your feet hip width apart with your toes facing outward. Gently contract your abdominal muscles to flatten your lower back into the surface. Attempt to maintain this gentle muscle contraction throughout the exercise.

2. Upward Phase: Gently exhale. Keep the abdominals engaged and lift your hips up. Press your heels into the surface for added stability. Avoid pushing your hips too high, as this can cause hyper extension (arching) in your lower back. Keeping your abdominals contracted helps to prevent excessive arching in the lower back.

3. Lowering Phase: Inhale and slowly lower yourself back to your starting position. Rest and repeat the exercise. Don't push yourself with this exercise, especially when first starting an exercise regimen.

Health and Well-Being

Musculature Disorders

The musculature system is comprised of the skeleton. This provides mechanical support and determines the shape of the muscles. The skeleton and muscle along with connective tissues power movement: such as tendons and ligaments, which hold the other components together.

The cartilage surfaces of the joints and the intervertebral discs of the spine allow for movement and flexibility.

Professional Drivers have a high risk of developing musculature disorders. This type of disorder affects the whole body, including our muscles, ligaments and tendons, as well as our bones. It is usually characterized by a stiffening pain that can be felt in the entire body. Your muscles may feel like they have been pulled or overworked. Similar to back pain, it is a particularly common stress factor for drivers.

Bus, lorry and taxi drivers are in their cabins for an extremely long period of time every working day, with little space for leg flexibility and movement. The restriction of movement leaves the body static, which aggravates muscular tension throughout the working day.

An extract from *European Agency for Safety and Health at Work; (2011) states the following:*

"Musculature risk are not just related to actual driving; the postural evaluation of the driver's workstation reveals a risk of musculature damage to the neck, created by the torsion/ twist movement made by driver when passengers get on and off the bus, along with

the extension movements made when looking at the central rear-view mirror during the opening and closing of the back doors."

Health and Well-Being

Taxi drivers imitate this type of movement whilst communicating with passengers when they give eye contact looking through the internal mirror.

Musculature complaints and disorders are also associated with exposure to intense whole body vibrations. This may occur if drivers regularly encounter poorly maintained roads where badly patched manholes, potholes and drain covers exist along a driver's assigned route.

This can be particularly hazardous for women drivers with fibroids and men drivers with gallstones.

Health and Well-Being

Pre-Surface for Drivers

A report from News.GOV.UK (9th March 2014) announced:

"The Government had made available extra money for repairs to local roads damaged by severe weather. Transport Secretary Patrick McLoughlin said, "The extra money is being distributed now to ensure that repairs can be started as soon as possible, so that the majority of the damage can be fixed ahead of the

summer holidays." A total of 116 local highway authorities in England will receive a share of the funding, along with a one-off payment to Transport for London to distribute to London Boroughs.

The Chancellor of the Exchequer announced in the March Budget that another £200 million will be provided for pothole repairs in financial year 2014-2015."

With this funding in place, drivers should report any road defects to their appropriate road safety department, ensuring their journeys are hazard free.

Same Road, Different Surface Since Road Repair Funding

This scheme is welcomed and seems to be making a big impact on the roads of London. Driving through the different towns, I have witnessed some major changes to roads and bus

stops. New bus stops and major foundation works are in progress.

An extract from *European Agency for Safety and Health at Work (2011)*

"The solutions are not only in the design of the cab. Additional measures can be taken to lessen the risk for both the shoulders and neck.

21

Health and Well-Being

For example:

- guaranteed breaks of at least ten minutes at the end of each journey, to allow the musculature system to adequately recuperate

- a reduction of driving hours, or a rotation of tasks between driving and other types of tasks

- drivers could also be trained to look after their musculature system by taking regular breaks along their routes and doing stretches and other exercises."

Musculature Disorders: Signs and Symptoms

People with muscle pain sometimes complain that their entire body aches. Their muscles may feel like they have been pulled or overworked. Sometimes, the muscles twitch or burn. Symptoms vary from person to person but the common symptoms are:

    a.   Pain
    b.   Fatigue
    c.   Sleep disturbances

Recommended Exercises With Illustrations

For added prevention of musculature conditions, the best exercises are the ones that work the whole body.

Star Exercises

Twirling Star

In the star position with belly button drawn

inward, turn your head to one side slowly and twist your entire spine, with your head looking at your hand. Relax while in this position breathing slowly in and out.

Return to the centre star position and turn your head to the other side, remembering to slowly twist your entire spine to the opposite side,

again with your head looking at your hand. Perform slowly three times on each side. Enjoy this slow, gentle stretch. Remember to breathe slowly and not over stretch.

NUTRITIONAL AID CHART

MAINTAINING THE HEALTH OF PROFESSIONAL DRIVERS

FRUITS	VEGETABLES	SNACKS	SMOOTHIES	HERBS/SUPPLEMENTS	FLUIDS
**Stress**					
Orange — Vitamin C is well known for boosting your immune system.	**Asparagus** — Is a mood enhancing nutrient with its high level of folic acid.	**Dark Chocolate** — Dark chocolate can help relieve stress at the molecular level.	**Blueberry** — Almond milk, fresh spinach, blueberry, frozen banana and flax seeds which help to restore energy.	**Kava Kava** — A herb from the South Pacific; a powerful muscle relaxant that helps to reduce depression.	**Liquorice Root Tea** — Contains a natural hormone alternative to cortisone, which can help the body when under stress.
**Back Pain**					
Tangerine — Filled with vitamin C and high in anti-inflammatory properties.	**Broccoli** — Vitamin K found in dark leafy vegetables help calcium deposit in the bones for strength.	**Pineapple** — Contains a host of very powerful enzymes that help the body heal. When purchasing, buy it fresh.	**Mixed Berries** — Strawberry, raspberry, blueberry acai berry, help the body control inflammation and aids the immune system.	**Gold Seal** — Aids both immune and antiseptic stimulatio by increasing blood flow to the spleen.	**Green Tea** — Drank regularly, it will help your cells protect the DNA from free radical damage.
**Musculature Disorder**					
Watermelon — Packed with antioxidants and glutathione which strengthen the immune system.	**Turnip** — Are a rich source of vitamins A, C and K.	**Almond** — Packed with B and E vitamins which boost the immune system.	**Green Vegetables** — Celery and lettuce both contain high amounts of k vitamins; add flaxseed oil for a juice boost.	**Dandelion** — Not just a weed but also a great herb for joint pain.	**Water** — Drinking ensures that your joints and muscles stay well lubricated and hydrated.
**Gastrointestinal Disorder**					
Apple — Bursting with pectin; research shows it benefits stomach and liver disorders.	**Celery** — Contain large amounts of cellulose which is beneficial in dieting.	**Walnut** — Are high in plantomega 3 and antioxidants.	**Aloe Vera** — Try adding 2 to 4 ounces to your daily protein shakes. This has multi health benefits including bowel movement.	**Digestive Enzymes** — Contai a mixture of enzymes that break down protein, carbohydrates and fats. Take with solid meals.	**Lemon Juice** — Lemon has anti-inflammatory effects which can kill bacteria, fungi and viruses in the body.
**Cardiovascular Disorder**					
Cherry — Packed with anthocyanins which are antioxidants believed to protect blood vessels.	**Carrot** — Is a top cholesterol fighting food with ample amounts of soluble fibre that assist in lowering heart disease.	**Almond** — Packed full of vitamin E, sterols, fibre and healthy fats that lowers cholesterol, reducing risk of diabetes.	**Avocado** — Avocado contain vitamins B6 and folic acid, providing heart support. Blueberries are full of antioxidants and disease fighting phytochemicals.	**Fresh Herbs** — Rosemary, sage, oregano and thyme contain antioxidants to fight heart disease.	**Tea and Coffee** — May help protect the heart as they ward off type 2 diabetes. Drinking 3 to 4 cups a day may cut the risk by 25%.

Be aware that the foods listed above may not be suitable for your personal health. Check with your doctor before consuming these supplements especially if using medication and be on the alert for any allergic reactions such as headache, nausea, dizziness or skin rashes.

Health and Well-Being

Twisting Star

From the star position, raise your arms in the hands up position. Bring your left elbow across your torso, raising your right leg.

Remain upright as you alternate to the other side. Repeat continously for up to 10 seconds.

Rest and repeat the exercise. Remember to inhale as you return to the start position and exhale while performing the stretch.

(Individuals with balance disorders should use caution attempting this exercise).

Tilting Star

Facing forward, spread your arms and legs outward into a star. Lean to the side from your hips, placing one hand in the air with the other hand at your side.

Slowly bend your entire spine as the lower hand reaches down the side of your thigh. Breathe in and out slowly while performing the exercise.

Remember, this is a stretch, so take your time! Repeat the sequence three times on each side, easy as you go.

25

Health and Well-Being

Gastrointestinal Disorders

Gastrointestinal disorders, commonly known as digestive diseases, are a group of diseases that affect the digestive system, which is composed of the mouth, oesophagus, gall bladder, stomach, small intestine, large intestine, anus, liver and pancreas. These organs are responsible for the digestion of food.

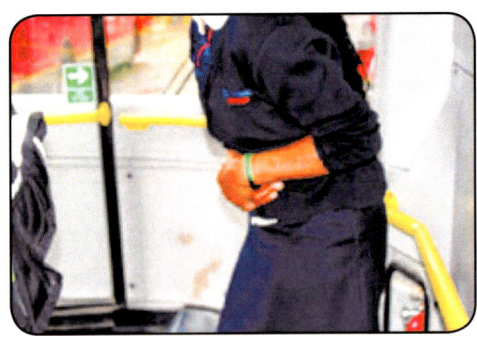

Drivers are more likely to experience higher levels of occupational risks than employees in other working groups. In fact, they are more at risk of suffering from blood vessel and

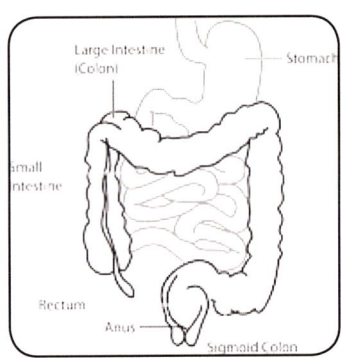

heart diseases, other cardiovascular ailments, musculature problems and gastrointestinal disorders than persons of other occupations. Professional driving demands maximum vigilance, concentration and swift reactions.

Driving is also associated with long, irregular hours of sitting at the wheel. The irregular driving schedules and strenuous working conditions are considered to be the major causes behind the gastrointestinal complaints of many drivers.

Other causes, such as the consumption of unhealthy snacks at work, irregular meal times and poor eating habits all put added pressure on the digestive system.

The occupational stress that drivers encounter can actually slow down the metabolism, which in the long run can trigger the development of gastrointestinal disorders. Stress is mostly derived from constant time pressure, traffic congestion, social isolation, irregular work schedules and even insufficient sleep or rest.

To Help Prevent Gastrointestinal Disorders

Meal times should be observed as regularly as possible, to ensure you are eating a balanced diet. Make sure that you have a good intake of

26

Health and Well-Being

healthy snacks throughout the day. This will keep your body nourished enough to manage the stress that may occur while driving. Ensure that you drink plenty of fluids to prevent dehydration.

Be aware of what you eat or drink and make sure that you do not overeat, as this will leave

you uncomfortable by creating more work for the digestive system. A Professional Driver's diet should include large amounts of cereals, grains, nuts, vegetables and fruits.

The driver should also be sure to do adequate physical activity when on a break. This is essential to help burn off food consumption. For example, stretch your entire body as you check the vehicle or do gentle yoga twisting exercises.

Recommended Exercises With Illustrations

The following gentle yoga exercises will help to balance your digestion. Yoga twists increase blood flow to the bowels and when followed by rest, help the movement of the bowels. The twists have also been shown to reduce inflammation and gastritis and strengthen the intestines.

Forward Folding

Stand tall with arms straight down and bend forward with your arms reaching up to the sky. Keep your back and legs as straight as you can without causing discomfort. Hold for 10 seconds. Resume the standing tall position and relax. Repeat this stretch 3 times.

Health and Well-Being

Standing Twist - Lunge with Arms in Prayer

Stand tall with your arms hanging at your sides. Gently lunge forward with your left foot in front.

Gently twist from the waist to the right and place your hands in prayer position, touching your right elbow to your left knee. Twist as far as possible, trying to maintain comfort and balance. Try holding for up to 10 seconds and repeat on the right side.

Repeat when well rested.

Standing Twist- Windmill Turn-Around

Stand with your legs shoulder width apart and with arms at your sides. Bend at the waist and place your right hand on your left foot, keeping

your back and legs as straight as possible. Twist your upper spine, raising your right hand to the sky until you feel the full stretch. Be sure to twist your head as you turn. Hold this stretch for 10 seconds.

Return to the upright position, relax and when ready repeat on the opposite side.

Repeat two times on both sides.

Health and Well-Being

Health and Well-Being

Cardiovascular Disorders

Cardiovascular disease (CVD)

A category of diseases of the heart and circulatory system that includes coronary heart disease, angina, heart attack, heart failure, congenital heart disease and stroke.

Coronary heart disease (CHD)

There are several main risk factors associated with the development of CHD and some studies have indeed corroborated that bus drivers are at a higher risk of developing CHD as a result of such factors.

Ischemic heart disease. This symptom is hardening of the coronary vessels; found to be greatest in drivers whose profiles fit that of the middle aged male between the ages of 50 and 59, is a consumer of cigarettes, obese, short in height and whose parents died between the ages of 40 and 64.

What increases the risk of cardiovascular disease?

There are several risk factors for CVD including:

Smoking
Diabetes
Ethnic background
High blood pressure
High blood cholesterol
Being physically inactive
Being overweight or obese
Family history of heart disease
Gender - men are more likely to develop CVD at an earlier age than women
Age - the older you are, the more likely you are to develop CVD

Cardiovascular disease and driving

Cardiovascular disease and driving have been linked, due to the high threat avoidance requirements (stress) of the job, where a high level of continued alertness needs to be maintained.

Social isolation and poor social support appear to aggravate cardiovascular disease as a result of increased job strain with no interaction with colleagues on the job.

Decreased control and low support, results in bus drivers having to follow guidelines which may not prove conducive to commuters, such as the **X68 Shuttle Service**, where commuters board with the intention of disembarking before the scheduled stops.

Health and Well-Being

With little control or support for the driver unnecessary stresses are created. These conflicting demands on the driver result from lack of proper research with inadequate input from the commuter. For instance, allowing passengers to get off at pick up stops, as it is a issue to the travellers, thereafter driving shuttle to the first intended station stop. Eliminating this expectation would prove conducive to the driver's health, as passengers are presently breaking the service regulation by demanding to disembark before scheduled stops. It would also eradicate a stress trigger, alleviating possible high blood pressure concerns for the driver.

Transport for London launched cashless payments on buses on 6th July 2014. It was good to see that TfL put in place an emergency oyster fare for travellers who had used up all their credit but were not aware. This move has decreased the stress on both commuter and driver, allowing for a workable transferable payment scheme.

Physiological reactions in bus drivers have been also documented. It is noted that time

pressures and impediments to the driver's journey, such as traffic congestion, creates stress, especially where time urgency is apparent because of road diversions or other factors.

Recommended Exercises With Illustrations

Tap Backs

To start tap backs, stand up straight with your feet shoulder width apart and arms straight

out. Step back with your right leg and swing both arms forward and repeat with the opposite leg in a continuous rhythmic movement. Look straight ahead and keep your hips and shoulders facing forward.

Don't let your front knee extend over your toes as you step back. Remember to keep your knees loose as you land. Your back heel needs to be off the floor at all times. Keep on the move, tapping back for 2 minutes.

Rest and repeat one more time.

Health and Well-Being

Single Leg Squat Thrust

Squat down comfortably, almost in a push up position, with your arms shoulder width apart and your feet and legs astride. If on a bus or coach, you can position yourself between the aisle seats. Keep your arms up at your sides with your palms placed on the seat surface.

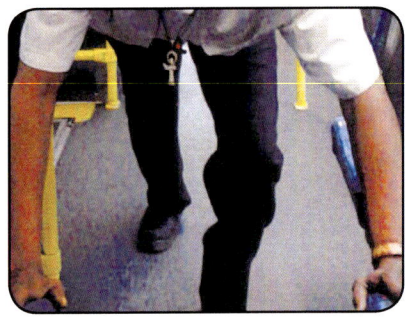

Thrust your left leg behind you to full extension. Use your arms to support you so that you are in a push up position. Keep your right leg in towards your hands, staying in the push up position, alternate legs so that your left leg is in front, with your right foot behind. Alternate

with the left right left right in a continuous and rhythmic movement. Make sure you are not pushing with your feet to bring your leg back up.

Continue this for 1 minute initially, ensuring to keep your back straight.

Rest well and repeat one more time.

Step Ups

Stand with both feet on one step and hold the hand rails for support and comfort. Place your left foot up one step and then move your right foot up to meet your left foot. Move your right foot back down and then move your left to meet it. Alternate and repeat with the opposite leg in a continuous rhythmic movement. Be sure to breathe in deeply and out slowly as you go.

Continue this for 1 minute initially. As you gain strength and endurance, you can increase

the time to 2 minutes.

Rest and repeat one more time.

CHAPTER 5

EATING HEALTHY AT WORK

Emotional Eating and Weight Gain

Emotional eating is a condition whereby we eat to feel better although we are not necessarily hungry; this is otherwise known as 'comfort eating'. The food we eat when comfort eating is usually not good for us, for the simple reason that we are not really hungry, so anything we eat will usually cause weight gain.

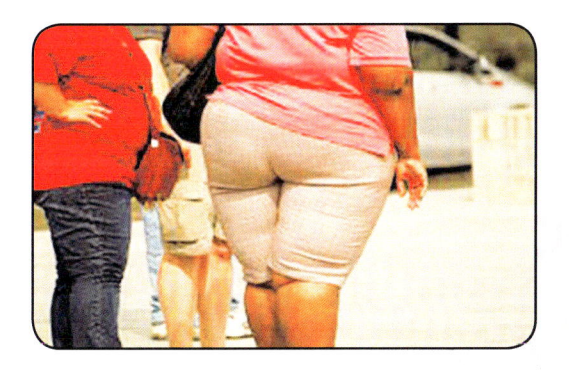

Emotional distress is the most common reason for comfort eating. It is estimated that 75% of overeating is caused by unstable emotions.

We all know that food can bring comfort. Consequently, we turn to food to heal emotional problems. As this spirals out of control, it prevents us from learning effective, healthy skills to resolve our emotional issues. Depression, boredom, loneliness, chronic anger, anxiety, frustration, stress, problems with interpersonal relationships or work colleagues and poor self-esteem are all emotional problems that can cause us to comfort eat or just overeat. One or more of these emotions may contribute to you becoming emotionally distressed.

By identifying what triggers the emotional eating, you can observe your moods and combat the urges. This will help you to have a more appropriate set of techniques in place to manage the emotional problems and take unhealthy food and weight gain out of the equation.

Identifying Eating Triggers

Situations and emotions that trigger us to eat fall into five main categories:

This eating trigger is a response to stress, fatigue, depression, boredom, tension, anger, anxiety and loneliness.

Health and Well-Being

Physiological

Physiological eating is a response to physical cues; for example eating more than you can eat because you feel you won't be getting another chance to eat.

Situational

This is eating because the opportunity exists; for example eating as it is time for your lunch break, although you're not hungry.

Social

Eating as a part of the ritual of socialising with other people or eating to fit in and be a part of a group.

Thoughts

Eating as a result of negative self-worth or making excuses for eating. You eat to feel better about yourself.

Identifying Emotional Eating

Observing the ways in which your bad eating habits are triggered is the first step to altering the behaviour. You will then need to observe your emotions when feeling the urge to eat. Determine if you are eating in response to emotions or certain situations. Ask yourself, "Am I really hungry?" "Can I not wait until lunch break?" "Is this a habit that I need to break?"

Emotional Eating Tips

Be strategic and have effective healthy alternatives in place. This will help you to overcome the triggers of emotional eating.

You could try replacing unhealthy eating with:

Essential oils - be sure to have your natural remedy by your side for a quick pick me up.

Deep breathing meditation exercises.

Healthy snacks, such as raw vegetables like carrots or celery, dried fruits, nuts and raisins. This will aid as a distraction until the urge to eat passes.

If you have tried but still require further help with excessive eating, try joining a group or activity in:
- Relaxation exercises
- Meditation
- Individual or group counselling

Correct Chewing For Your Digestive System

Healthy eating habits are a vital part of wellness throughout your working life into retirement. The chewing process serves as the first step in proper digestion, as properly chewed food is easier to digest. Chewing breaks down food particles. It is recommended that food should be chewed until there are no more chunks before swallowing. This exposes the food to your saliva, which is important, as your saliva is composed of enzymes that help the digestive system break food down once in your stomach. This allows the nutrients of the meal to be absorbed so your body can easily convert them into energy.

The effects of not properly breaking down food

Health and Well-Being

before swallowing causes less enzymes to be created and an increased gas formation of wind, (which can damage the lining). This results in your stomach having to work harder to break down the food, leading to a bloated stomach feeling and possible eventual blockage of the colon and other digestive problems.

So what are some benefits of chewing your food thoroughly?

- It helps start the important digestive process, which is important to staying healthy.
- It aids in the proper transport of nutrients in your body.
- You are more likely to eat less, by chewing thoroughly.
- Helps to prevent the heavy feeling that sometimes follows a meal.
- Will help you lose body fat since you are not eating as much.
- Chewing each mouthful thoroughly allows less air to enter, resulting in decreased gas formation and burping.

What are some of the side effects of not chewing thoroughly?

- Less of the vitamins and nutrients that the foods have to offer are extracted and absorbed by your body.
- Eating quickly and swallowing large mouthfuls contribute to acid reflux, which can damage the lining of the throat and oesophagus.
- Flatulence, indigestion, heartburn, gas, irritable bowel syndrome (IBS) and other discomforts.

Health and Well-Being

Microwave Reheating Good or Bad? You Decide!

The Microwave Oven Era

Unlike most inventions that took painstaking researching, testing and convincing before becoming a viable product, the microwave oven was fortunate to avoid all these stages. Apparently in the 1940s Mr. Percy Spencer from the United States, a self-taught engineer, noticed that a chocolate bar he had in his pocket started to melt, whilst he was building radar equipment in a lab for Raytheon. He had been building magnetrons and realised that microwaves can be directed at food to heat it up rapidly. This started the microwave oven era. The product soon grew in popularity all over the world. Then some 30 years later, in 1976, the Soviet Union temporarily banned the use of microwave ovens in their country. They were by this time already being used all around the globe.

Heated Plastics in a Microwave Can Be Dangerous

With recession biting, a large number of drivers bring meals into work which need to be reheated before they can tuck into an enjoyable meal. However I am concerned to see that up to 80% of Professional Drivers are either ignoring the fact, or are not aware, that they should only be reheating using microwave safe containers.

Reports have suggested that if plastic containers containing chemical phthalates and BPA are heated in the microwave, these chemicals may migrate into the food.

I have witnessed drivers reheating meals in various types of plastic containers. This alerted me to the alarming fact that drivers may be unaware that they are sacrificing their health by using the wrong containers in the microwave. Many plastics have been found to release toxic doses of Bisphenol A when heated in a microwave. In tests, lab rats could not endure the chemical reactions; they proved fatal. When considering the risk, why use any type of plastic at all?

The safest course of action is to avoid putting any plastics in the microwave. Consider using a food thermos instead. They have been around for a considerable length of time and have a natural way of keeping food hot by the use of boiling hot water in a sealed compartment.

Health and Well-Being

There are a limited number of studies that may suggest otherwise but given the lack of large scale or compelling evidence, it's hard to feel that tossing out your microwave is a particularly necessary step. There is however, a saying that 'prevention is better than cure' and as wise old men always say, "take time to know."

It is your decision - YES or NO?

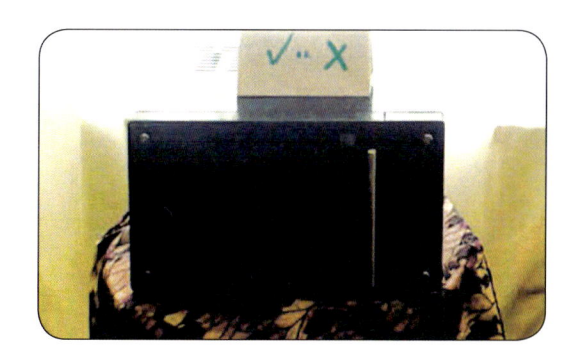

In fact the microwave oven has been criticised for not heating food evenly, sometimes leaving cold pockets next to hot pockets, making the meal prone to bacteria. Have you experienced this?

In the medical profession it has been reported that microwaving human blood renders it unsafe for transfusion, though medical professionals point out that rapidly heating blood via any method can have the same negative result.

However, the conclusion by Government agencies and independent organisations is that microwaved food is safe, as well as convenient.

CHAPTER 6

SOCIAL HEALTH & ADDICTION

Cigarette Smoking and Alcohol

In the past, alcohol and smoking were seen as ways of socialising - something extra to do during times of social enjoyment. Today we smoke and drink more for stress relief, to help maintain a calm state or to help us unwind. It has been observed that drivers have a tendency to smoke more and consume more alcohol, the longer they stay in the transportation industry. It has been noted that there is a converse relationship between consumption and job satisfaction. Job stresses, either on the road or with colleagues, contribute to driver's excessive usage.

The addictive level of alcohol linked it globally as the third leading cause of disease and disability, after child malnutrition and unprotected sex. Excessive alcohol consumption is known to cause many serious health problems, including the development of 60 major types of disease and approximately 2.5 million deaths per year, more than HIV or tuberculosis.

The most critical factor about drinking alcohol is its correlation with the decisions a person makes after consuming it, as drinking alters people's perceptions tremendously. It pacifies the consumer, creating a false sense of control. The fact is that drinking alcohol is known to reduce inhibitions, as individuals are more inclined to take risks while under its influence. The high risk factor from drinking and driving is well known. It lowers concentration levels, creates a sense of lethargy and increases the likelihood of accidents.

Cigarettes are highly addictive, with over 4,000 chemicals found in the average cigarette. The purpose of some of these chemicals is to stimulate addiction, which increases the urge to smoke more frequently.

Cigarette smoking and inhalation are linked with numerous diseases and ailments, some of which are linked with alcohol consumption. Among these are cardiovascular diseases such as abdominal aortic aneurysm, cerebrovascular disease and coronary heart disease. Known reproductive effects include reduced female fertility, premature delivery, foetal death and low birth weight. Cancers of the bladder, cervix, oesophagus, kidney and lungs are also linked with cigarette smoking and smoke inhalation.

Stressful situations are worsened by alcohol and cigarettes as they bring about a false sense of security. Assess your emotional state the next time you feel a craving for alcohol or a cigarette. Try to identify the type of stress you are feeling. It will fall into one of two categories - those that reside primarily **outside the person** and those that are more **within the person**. Stressors outside the person include difficult work environments, economic pressures or personal change. Factors within the individual that influence stress consists of patterns of thinking and acting, unrealistic expectations and personality disorders. Having assessed your feelings, do you really need to have this one? Challenge the urge by doing some exercise or eating something healthy instead, or just allow yourself some 'quiet time', even if it's just a few minutes.

Although the driving industry is highly stressful, it is possible that by using harm reduction strategies, you can make the choice to consume alcohol in moderation and not experience any short or long term ill effects.

Smoking fewer cigarettes will increase your energy, as your blood circulation will improve and your immune system will also be more equipped to fight off infections. Help is always close by.

(G-AL) Bus Talk (Issue 26) excerpt report:

"Merton garage urge staff to give it up! On January 17th 2014 they had a nurse attend the garage to talk not only about the dangers of smoking, but also how people could give it up. Employees were offered the chance to sign up to a programme designed to help them stop smoking once and for all. With many people attending and five people signing up to the programme, it showed the need for this visit. Due to the success of this visit more have been booked for March 28th and then every three months after that."

This is another way in which G-AL shows their commitment to staff health and well-being.

Many years ago, the risks of drinking and smoking were unknown. Fortunately, today we are well informed and research has clearly exposed the negative side effects of alcohol consumption and cigarette smoking.

Alcohol and Drug Consumption

Alcohol Consumption

Professional Drivers need to always be aware of the implications of drinking. The level of units consumed in each alcoholic drink should be monitored in order to avoid exceeding the limit. Did you know that even the following day you could be prohibited from driving, if you consumed too many units with insufficient clear time for the alcohol to leave your system? It is imperative to understand how to evaluate the units in each given drink and the different rates at which they will work through your system. You may feel sober the following day but that does not mean you are legally fit to drive. Drivers need to adopt the notion that regardless of the legal limit, the desirable level of alcohol to consume on the day preceding a working day, is zero.

Prescribed Drugs or Over the Counter Medications

Professional Drivers need to assess their ability to drive once they have taken prescribed drugs, or over the counter medications. They need to observe the prescribed regulated dose and ensure they do not go over the limit.

Health and Well-Being

They need to be aware of the legal requirements pertaining to prescribed drugs or over the counter medications when driving. Drivers need to assess their ability to drive safely; ensuring competence has not been affected by the dose taken, despite adhering to the recommended dosage. Ensure that you are not feeling drowsy, over anxious or restless.

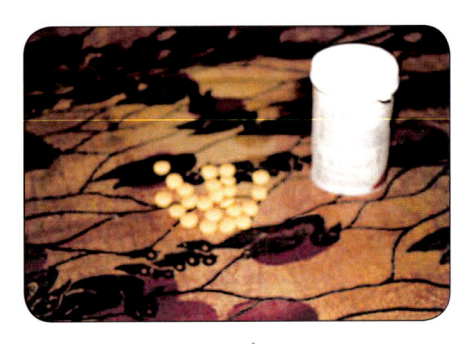

Street Drugs / Illegal Substances

Professional Drivers should never have any type of street drugs / illegal substances in their bloodstream. They must be cognizant of the fact that their emotional state is adversely affected by the use of drugs. Awareness of the risks linked with illegal substances and driving, particularly how it impinges on one's ability to drive competently and not endanger other road users and pedestrians, is critical knowledge for the Professional Driver. It is essential that they understand how the body processes drugs, knowing that the body retains proof of drugs in the bloodstream, saliva and hair. Random testing is ongoing in many establishments. Driving under the influence of drugs or alcohol can cause Professional Drivers to lose their lucrative license; bus drivers will also lose their free public transport facility.

Seek Help Now

As an employee for G-AL, London and Central Bus Company, I have been given the policy on illegal substances within my contract of employment. All professional driving establishments must by law have a policy on drugs and alcohol and illegal substance use and hand it out to their employees.

If you feel your drinking, cigarette smoking or use of prescribed or over the counter drugs are spiralling out of control, or if you are a user of street drugs, you need to seek help NOW. Talking to someone TODAY should be your FIRST course of action. Talk with your employer today; they will give you support to break the habit and help you get back behind the wheel safely.

The DSA state in their **'Performance Standards'**.

"Follow your organisation's procedures when you are legally unable to drive."

If you want privacy with your addiction, anonymity is protected through most Narcotics or Alcoholics Anonymous services. Private as well as Government run provisions are also available to the public. Freedom Recovery Services for addiction (www. freedomrecoverycentre.co.uk), is located in Catford, South East London. Most services will offer a phone assessment. Programs can consist of medicated detox, psychological support, counselling and talking therapies.

If in doubt, make use of the resources. Remember the HIGH IMPLICATIONS!!

Health and Well-Being

CHAPTER 7

CONCLUSION

In compiling this manual for Professional Driver's Health, it has been my aim to provide drivers with an overview of common ailments associated with professional driving and the reasons for them. Constructive exercises to ease and prevent the discussed ailments, along with nutrients that can heal and prevent illnesses have also been included.

In exploring the transportation industry's input into drivers' health, it is clear that for over 50 years this business has been zealous in contributing services, appliances, painstaking research and working with associated companies to analyse all areas of this dilemma; helping to create a healthier work environment for Professional Drivers.

My findings are that Professional Drivers can avoid becoming injured or ill from the industry's most common occupational hazards. This leads me to suggest that drivers need to adopt far greater active measures in sustaining their health and that inadequate information may have unintentionally contributed to the current health problems with surface drivers. It is apparent that for many years Professional Drivers have not been motivated in addressing their health, this has now progressed into an unhealthy situation.

It is apparent that employers need to take the leading role, being assertive in encouraging a healthier work force.

The scale of the current health problems exhibited by Professional Surface Drivers is fundamentally obvious, as there seems to be an undisputed trend. Many readers will need weaning into adopting some of the healthy changes needed, not only for the driver's well-being but also for the health and safety of their passengers, other road users and their cargo. It is my aim that DSA 2014 whose name recently changed to Driving and Vehicle Standards Agency (DaVSA) along with TfL and G-AL will all have vital central roles in equipping drivers with this manual.

Health and Well-Being

SUGGESTED READING LIST

Whitelegg, J (May 1995). *Health of Professional Drivers*. A Report for Transport & General Workers Union.© Eco-Logica Ltd 1995
www.eco-logica.co.uk/pdf/HealthProDrivers

Driving Standards Agency. National standard for driving buses and coaches (category D)™ Version 2.0 (March 2013). Element 1.1.1. Make sure you are fit to drive pg3-4 gov.uk Publication
https://www. gov.uk/government/organisations/driving-standards-agency

Go-Ahead London Bus Talk issue 26

Gov.uk. *Councils receive share of roads repair funding*.https://www.gov.uk

The European Agency for Safety and Health at Work (EU-OSHA). Occupational Safety and *Health of Road Transport Drivers* 12 Santiago de Compostela (EdificioMiribilla), 5th Floor E-48003 Bilbao, SPAINhttps://osha.europa.eu/en/sector /road_transport/index_html.

Kompier, M.A.J. (1996). Bus drivers: *Occupational stress and stress prevention*. Department of Work and Organizational Psychology, University of Nijmegen

http://www.bus driver occupational stress prevention

REFERENCES

Alperovltch-Najenson, D, Santo, Y, Masharawl, Y, Katz-Leurer, M., Ushvaev, D, Kalichman, L. (2010). *Low back pain among professional bus drivers: ergonomic and occupational-psychosocial* riskfactors.www .ncbl.nlm.nlh.gov[accessed 23/04/13]

Atlas Ergonomics. *Supporting your investment in* people.www.atlasergo.com[accessed 20/07/13]

Ausnaturalcare. *Constipation:10 tips to help get your bowels* moving.www.ausnaturalcare.com [accessed 14/3/13]

Driving Ergonomics. www.ergonomicssimplified com/tips/driving [accessed 09/07/13]

Driving Standards Agency. National standard for driving buses and coaches (category D)Version 2.0 (March 2013). Element 1.1.1. Make sure you are fit to drive pg3-4 gov.uk Publication www.gov.uk/ government/organisations/driving-standards-agency [accessed 25/03/13]

Exercising when you have a gastrointestinal disorder. www.webmd. com [accessed 18/04/13]

EddieJackman. *How to Adjust your Seating Position while Driving - pt* 1www.eddleJackman.com [accessed 24/09/13]

Everyday *Health. Identify Your Emotioal Eating* Triggerswww.everydayhealth.com [accessed 25/06/13]

Go-Ahead London (Bus Talk Issue 26- February 2014). *Staff get on their bikes!- Staff urged to give it up!- kicking the habit.*

Gov.uk. *Councils receive share of roads repair funding.* www.Gov.uk [accessed 28/03/14]

Helpgulde.org. *Emotional Eating*,www.helpgulde.org [accessed 23/06/13]

How to Reduce Stress. 10 Relaxation Techniques. www.webmd.com [accessed 20/06/14]

How to *Adjust Seating to the Proper Position While* Driving.http://www.wikihow.com/ [accessed 28/10/13]

John L.M. Tse, RhonaFlin, Kathryn MearnsBus *driver well-being review.* 50 years of research www. high demands, low control, and low support for bus drivers [accessed 03 12/12]

Kompler, M.A.J. (1996). *Bus drivers: Occupational stress and stress prevention.* www.bus driver occupational stress prevention [accessed 25/09/12]

MacKechnie, Christopher. (March 6, 2013). Bus Driver Health.www.publictransport.about.com. [accessed 25/05/13]

Mayo Clinic, Exercise: 7benefits of regular physical activity. Back exercises in 15 minutes a day. www. mayoclinic.org [accessed 23/05/13]

MohdKhairir Bin Ismai. (April 2010). *Ergonomics Design and Analysis of Bus Driver Seat Faculty of Mechanical Engineering.* www.Erogonmics+Design+and+Analaysis+of+Bus+Driver+Seat [accessed 17/05/12]

Health and Well-Being

National centre for eating disorders. *Compulsive Overeating & Binge Eating Disorder*. http://stress.about.com [accessed 27/7/13]

NHS Choices *Cardiovascular-Disease*.www.wikipedia.org/wiki/Cardiovascular_disease [accessed 23/08/12]

NHS Choices. *Exercise to relieve stress*.http://www.nhs.uk [accessed 25/06/13]

Petch, M. C. (1998). *Driving and heart* disease. Prepared on behalf of the Task Force European Heart Journal. www.escardio.org guidelines-policyconf-cvd-driving-ft-1998 [accessed 05/08/12]

Posture Medic. *Driving posture.posturemedic.com* [accessed 20/09/12]

Precision Nutrition. *All About Microwave Cooking*. www.precisionnutrition.com [accessed 18/05/12]

Revive life Clinic. *Top 5 Exercises For Digestive Health*.www.revivelifeclinic.com [accessed 23/05/13]

11 Surprising Facts and Myths about Microwave Ovens www.goodhousekeeping.com [accessed 23/08/13]

Straighten up UK *Straighten up UK three minute posture care leaflet*. www.straightenupuk.org

The European Agency for Safety and Health at Work (EU-OSHA}. *Occupational Safety and Health of Road Transport Drivers* www.osha.europa road_transport[accessed 18/10/12]

Tse, John L.M., Flin, Rhona, Mearns, Kathryn.'Bus-ting' a *gut- the strains of an urban bus driver. www.*abdn.ac.uk/Bus-ting [accessed 19/05/13]

Tse, John L.M., Flin,Rhona, Mearns, Kathryn. (2006). Transportation Research Part F 9 *Bus driver well being review*: 50 years of research, www.bus_driver_wellbeing.pdf [accessed 18/04/13]

Whitelegg, J. (May 1995). *Health of Professional Drivers*. A Report for Transport & General Workers Union. www.eco-logica.co.uk/pdf/HealthProDrivers [accessed 18/3/13]

Winkleby, M.A., Ragland, D.R., Fisher, J.M., Syme, S.L. (17 June 1988). Excess *Risk of Sickness and Disease in Bus Drivers*, www.ncbi.nlm.nih.gov/pubmed [accessed 14/05/12]